CREDO ◆

A Catholic Prayer Book

Unless otherwise noted, Scripture quotations are from the Revised Standard Version of the Bible—Second Catholic Edition (Ignatius Edition), copyright © 2006 National Council of the Churches of Christ in the United States of America. Used by permission. All rights reserved.

Cover and interior design by Caroline Green

ISBN: 978-1-5051-1161-3

Published in the United States by
Saint Benedict Press
PO Box 410487
Charlotte, NC 28241
www.SaintBenedictPress.com

Printed in the United States of America

I BELIEVE...

Contents

PART V: PRAYERS FOR PARTICULAR TIMES

PART VI: PRAYERS FOR PARTICULAR NEEDS

INTRODUCTION

The Spirit helps us in our weakness; for we do not know how to pray as we ought, but the Spirit himself intercedes for us with sighs too deep for words.

—ROMANS 8:26

This book is a companion piece to the RCIA program *Credo* and has been compiled to introduce catechumens and candidates to the wealth of Catholic devotional prayers. Far from being exhaustive, this book is meant to offer a representative sampling of the most common vocal prayers said by Catholics. While it was originally composed for *new* Catholics, it can certainly be used by any Catholic to assist and nurture one's prayer life.

The first section, *Basic Prayers*, includes the kind of prayers that all Catholics should ideally know by memory. The best way to memorize them is to begin praying them on a daily basis. The second section, *Guides*, serves as a "how to" and offers readers guidance on confession and how to say the Rosary and Divine Mercy Chaplet. The third section, *Marian Prayers*, provides some of the most well-known petitions to Our Lady, while the fourth section, *Saint Prayers*, offers examples of prayers *to* saints as well as prayers composed *by* saints. The fifth section, *Prayers for Particular Times*, offers prayers for particular times throughout the day and prayers to be said before and after receiving Holy Communion. In the sixth section, *Prayers for Particular Needs*, readers will find the voice and words to match particular occasions. The seventh section, *Novenas and Litanies*, is meant to introduce readers to a sample of prayers said on nine successive days (novenas) and collections of short invocations (litanies). Finally, at the end readers will find a miscellaneous group titled *Other Prayers* that may not fall into one of the categories but are nonetheless helpful to know and pray. Due to the nature of some prayers, they may be found in multiple categories.

Following these groups of prayers is a brief compendium of various important lists and other information, such as the Ten Commandments, the Beatitudes, the Precepts of the Church, and others.

PART I

Basic Prayers

THE SIGN OF THE CROSS

IN THE NAME of the Father, and of the Son, and of the Holy Spirit. Amen.

OUR FATHER

OUR FATHER, Who art in Heaven, hallowed be Thy Name. Thy kingdom come, Thy will be done on earth as it is in Heaven. Give us this day our daily bread, and forgive us our trespasses, as we forgive those who trespass against us. And lead us not into temptation, but deliver us from evil. Amen.

HAIL MARY

HAIL MARY, full of grace, the Lord is with thee; blessed art thou among women, and blessed is the fruit of thy womb, Jesus. Holy Mary, Mother of God, pray for us sinners, now and at the hour of our death. Amen.

GLORY BE

GLORY BE to the Father, and to the Son, and to the Holy Spirit. As it was in the beginning, is now, and ever shall be, world without end. Amen.

THE NICENE CREED

I BELIEVE in one God,
the Father almighty,
maker of heaven and earth,
of all things visible and invisible.
I believe in one Lord Jesus Christ,
the Only Begotten Son of God,
born of the Father before all ages.

God from God, Light from Light,
true God from true God,
begotten, not made, consubstantial with
the Father;
through him all things were made.
For us men and for our salvation
he came down from heaven,
and by the Holy Spirit was incarnate of the
Virgin Mary,
and became man.
For our sake he was crucified under Pontius
Pilate,
he suffered death and was buried,
and rose again on the third day
in accordance with the Scriptures.
He ascended into heaven
and is seated at the right hand of the
Father.
He will come again in glory
to judge the living and the dead
and his kingdom will have no end.
I believe in the Holy Spirit, the Lord,
the giver of life,

who proceeds from the Father and the Son,
who with the Father and the Son
  is adored and glorified,
who has spoken through the prophets.
I believe in one, holy, catholic and apostolic
  Church.
I confess one Baptism for the forgiveness of
  sins
and I look forward to the resurrection
  of the dead
and the life of the world to come. Amen.

THE APOSTLES' CREED

I believe in God, the Father Almighty,
Creator of Heaven and earth; and in Jesus
Christ, His only Son Our Lord, Who was
conceived by the Holy Spirit, born of the
Virgin Mary, suffered under Pontius Pilate,
was crucified, died, and was buried.
He descended into Hell; the third day He
rose again from the dead; He ascended into
Heaven, and sitteth at the right hand of

God, the Father almighty; from t
shall come to judge the living and th.
I believe in the Holy Spirit, the holy
olic Church, the communion of saint:
forgiveness of sins, the resurrection of
body and life everlasting. Amen.

COME, HOLY SPIRIT

V. Come, Holy Spirit, fill the hearts of Thy
faithful;

R. *And kindle in them the fire of Thy love.*

V. Send forth Thy Spirit, and they shall be
created;

R. *And Thou shalt renew the face of the earth.*

Let Us Pray

O God, Who has instructed the hearts of
the Faithful by the light of the Holy Spirit,
grant we beseech Thee, that by the gift of
the same Spirit we may be always truly wise
and ever rejoice in His consolation, through
Christ Our Lord. Amen.

C PRAYERS

ence He
dead.
Cath-
the
he

ve that Thou art
Persons: the Father,
y Spirit. I believe that
ecame man, and died for
at He shall come to judge the
ne dead. I believe these and all
s which the Holy Catholic Church
es, because Thou has revealed them,
no can neither deceive nor be deceived.

THE ACT OF HOPE

O MY GOD, relying on Thy almighty power and infinite mercy and promises, I hope to obtain pardon of my sins, the help of Thy grace, and life everlasting, through the merits of Jesus Christ, my Lord and Redeemer.

THE ACT OF CHARITY

O MY GOD, I love Thee above all things, with my whole heart and soul, because Thou art all-good and worthy of all love. I love my neighbor as myself for the love of Thee. I forgive all who have injured me, and ask pardon of all whom I have injured.

SALVE REGINA (HAIL, HOLY QUEEN)

HAIL, holy Queen, Mother of mercy, our life, our sweetness and our hope! To thee do we cry, poor banished children of Eve. To thee do we send up our sighs, mourning and weeping in this valley of tears. Turn then, Most Gracious Advocate, thine eyes of mercy toward us. And after this our exile, show unto us the blessed Fruit of thy womb, Jesus. O clement, O loving, O sweet Virgin Mary.

LEADER: Pray for us O Holy Mother of God

RESPONSE: That we may be made worthy of the promises of Christ.

THE MEMORARE

REMEMBER, O most gracious Virgin Mary, that never was it known that anyone who fled to thy protection, implored thy help or sought thy intercession was left unaided. Inspired with this confidence, I fly unto thee, O Virgin of virgins, my Mother. To thee do I come, before thee I stand, sinful and sorrowful. O Mother of the Word Incarnate, despise not my petitions, but in thy mercy hear and answer me. Amen.

GUARDIAN ANGEL PRAYER

ANGEL of God, my guardian dear, To whom God's love commits me here, Ever this day (night), be at my side, To light and guard, to rule and guide. Amen.

PRAYER TO ST. MICHAEL THE ARCHANGEL

ST. MICHAEL the Archangel, defend us in the battle; be our protection against the wickedness and snares of the devil. May God rebuke him, we humbly pray, and do thou, O Prince of the heavenly host, by the power of God, cast into Hell Satan and all the other evil spirits who prowl about the world seeking the ruin of souls. Amen.

GRACE BEFORE MEALS

BLESS US, O Lord, and these Thy gifts which we are about to receive from Thy bounty, through Christ Our Lord. Amen.

GRACE AFTER MEALS

WE GIVE Thee thanks, Almighty God, for these and all Thy benefits, Who live and reign forever. Amen.

ACT OF CONTRITION

O MY GOD, I am heartily sorry for having offended Thee, and I detest all my sins because I dread the loss of Heaven and the pains of Hell; but most of all, because they offend Thee, my God, Who art all good and deserving of all my love. I firmly resolve, with the help of Thy grace, to confess my sins, to do penance and to amend my life. Amen.

— PART II —

GUIDES

HOW TO GO TO CONFESSION

Jesus knew that sin would continue to remain a problem even for the baptized, so he instituted a solution to treat the weakness and sinfulness of his members. He entrusted the forgiveness of sins to the Church and gave us the sacrament of confession as one of his great channels of grace.

After the Resurrection, Our Lord entrusted to his apostles the power to forgive sins in his name: "He breathed on them, and said to them, 'Receive the Holy Spirit. If you forgive the sins of any, they are forgiven; if you retain the sins of any, they are retained'" (Jn 20:22–24). Through apostolic succession and Holy Orders, bishops and priests receive the power to forgive sins. The sacrament of confession exists principally so that those who commit serious sins at some point after their baptism can be reconciled with God and restored to the life of grace and holiness. The sacrament of confession is also called the sacrament of Reconciliation because it *reconciles* a sinner with God and the Church.

Before approaching the sacrament of confession, it is important to understand something about sin. Sin is essentially an offense against God. It can be a thought, a word, or an action we do (sin of commission) or neglect to do (sin of omission). But not all sins are of the same severity. A mortal sin is a serious offense against God, a grave violation of his law. Mortal sin takes its name from the word *death*. Like a mortal wound, mortal sin causes spiritual death to the soul. A mortal sin is a grave violation of God's law (a sin concerning something serious, called "grave matter") that one commits with full knowledge and complete consent. A mortal sin may also be called a "grave" or "serious" sin. Mortal sin kills supernatural charity (the love of God that is supernaturally infused into the soul by grace) because every mortal sin involves choosing to act in disobedience to God's command to love him (since sin, at its core, is loving something else more than God). A venial sin is when one fails to observe the moral law through a lesser offense. If someone commits a gravely serious action but without full knowledge of what he is doing or without consent of the will, the sin is also venial.

To some, going to confession might seem daunting or even intimidating, but it is helpful to remember that it is a tremendous gift of mercy. Through this sacrament, God will help you to be free of the burden of sin. In fact, God will give you the strength to make a good confession. And when, with God's help, you acknowledge your sins directly and make an act of repentance for them, God gives the wonderful gift of true and complete forgiveness for them.

Preparing for Confession

Before going to confession, it is important to do an examination of conscience; that is, to take time to reflect and remember what sins we may have committed since our last confession. There are many different guides available that can help you make a good examination of conscience, and we have provided one here for you as well. Most guides go through the different types of sin according to the Ten Commandments. Doing an examination of conscience helps one articulate and express his sins honestly and thoroughly. It is a time to allow God to begin his healing work in our souls and to prepare us for the grace of the sacrament.

Some may be concerned that they do

not remember absolutely *all* of their sins. This is okay. God only asks that we express our sins as best as we can remember them. The sacrament forgives even those sins we forget to confess. After confession, if more sins come to mind from the past that you honestly forgot to mention, simply include them in your next confession.

As a sacrament, confession is a part of the liturgy (our public worship of God), and so it has a set ritual form; meaning, it is more than a casual conversation. This gives it structure and helps make it a prayerful encounter with God's mercy. At the same time, it does allow you to ask questions and speak back and forth in a conversational way with the priest. You should feel comfortable talking with the priest and asking him a question if you need. If you are unsure of what to do or how you should say something, just ask. You should also feel free to ask questions relating to your sins and to living out the Catholic faith. So don't worry about "forgetting your lines." If there is a part you are supposed to say, like the Act of Contrition prayer, but forget, the priest will walk you through it.

Going to Confession

1. Go into the confessional, make the sign of the cross, and say aloud "In the name of the Father, and of the Son, and of the Holy Spirit." Then say: "**Bless me Father it has been (name the time: two weeks, a month, a year, etc.) since my last confession.**" Also say your state in life so the priest knows the context of your sins. For example, "**I am married,**" "**I am single,**" "**I am engaged to be married,**" etc.

2. Name your sins. The order you confess your sins in does not matter, but it can be a good idea to start with the hard ones just to get them out of the way. If you have committed any mortal sins, say what they are and (as best you can)

PART II : GUIDES

how many times you have committed them. For example, "I missed Sunday Mass twice without a serious reason to do so." Or "I have viewed pornographic materials twice a week for the last several weeks." Confess the venial sins you are aware of, too. You do not need to mention how many times you committed a venial sin, but you can if you want.

3. When you are done saying all the sins you can remember say, **"For these and any sins I may have forgotten I am truly sorry."** Or you might say, **"For these and all the sins of my life, I am sincerely sorry."**

4. The priest will usually give you some advice and may ask you to clarify some things to help you make a good and thorough confession. This is normal. You may also ask the priest questions related to your sins.

17

5. The priest will eventually give you a "penance," for example, some prayers to say. Then, the priest will invite you to say an act of contrition (found in this book). The Act of Contrition helps you manifest your sorrow.

6. Say an act of contrition. There are many different ones, but this is most common: *O my God, I am heartily sorry for having offended You. I detest all my sins because I dread the loss of heaven and the pains of hell. But most of all because they offend You, my God, who are all good and deserving of all my love. I firmly resolve, with the help of Your grace to sin no more and to avoid the near occasions of sin. Amen.*

The Act of Contrition should eventually be committed to memory. If you cannot remember it, ask the priest to help you make one or remember to bring a written copy of it.

7. The priest will give you absolution with the formula of absolution. This beautiful prayer ends with "I absolve you from your sins in the name of the Father, and of the Son, and of the Holy Spirit" to which you respond "Amen."

8. The priest will end with some short concluding words. Although it is typically not necessary, you may respond "Amen" or "Thanks be to God."

9. After confession, you may breathe a sigh of relief knowing that your sins have been forgiven. You can take a short time to pray and offer thanks to God for his mercy.

10. Remember to perform your penance! Your sins are forgiven by the absolution, but your penance is still an important part of the sacrament and must be completed.

EXAMINATION OF CONSCIENCE

1. **"I am the LORD your God. . . . You shall
   have no other gods before me" (Ex
   20:2 –3).**

   **"You shall love the LORD your God with
   all your heart, and with all your soul,
   and with all your might" (Dt 6:5).**

   Do I pray every day?

   Do I strive to have a personal relation-
   ship of love with God?

   Does God truly hold the first place in my
   life?

   Do I "compartmentalize" God in my life?
   Am I a Christian on Sundays but something else during the week?

   Do I believe what God has revealed and
   profess the Catholic faith wholeheart-
   edly? Do I accept the Church's teaching?

   Do I search for answers to my questions
   about the Faith or do I cultivate a spirit
   of disbelief?

Have I avoided dangers to my faith?

"Where your treasure is, there will your heart be also" (Lk 12:34).

Do I place undue value and time on gaining and possessing those things the world considers important?

Am I materialistic in my attitude and outlook in regard to money?

Have I participated in the occult, witch-craft, fortune telling, ouija boards, seances, tarot cards? Have I engaged in superstitious practices? Have I actually believed in horoscopes?

Have I committed any sacrileges?

Have I received Holy Communion in a state of mortal sin?

Have I told a lie in confession or deliberately withheld confessing a mortal sin? (If so, make sure to confess all the sins you can remember since your last good confession.)

Have I ever denied a truth of the Catholic faith out of embarrassment?

Have I ever despaired of God's love for me?

Have I committed the sin of presumption by presuming that God would forgive me after committing a sin?

2. **You shall not take the name of the Lord your God in vain.**

Have I insulted God's holy name or used it lightly or carelessly?

Have I spoken any blasphemies against God or the saints?

Have I used foul or inappropriate language?

Have I wished evil on anyone?

3. **Remember to keep holy the Lord's day.**

Have I missed Mass on Sundays or holy days of obligation without a serious reason (for example: illness, impossibility due to severe weather)?

Do I show God indifference by not taking Mass seriously? Do I leave early or come late deliberately or without good reason?

The Sabbath is a day of solemn rest, holy to the Lord (cf. Ex 31:15). Have I avoided unnecessary servile work on Sundays?

4. Honor your father and your mother.

Do I honor and obey my parents?

Have I cursed at my parents or harmed them in any way?

Do I honor and obey my legitimate superiors?

Have I neglected my family responsibilities?

5. You shall not kill.

Have I deliberately hurt anyone?

Have I had an abortion? Have I encouraged or assisted anyone in any way to have an abortion?

Have I abused drugs or alcohol?

Do I have unresolved hatred, anger, or resentment? (Feel free to talk through this with the priest.)

Have I given scandal to anyone by my sins, thereby leading them to sin?

Have I deliberately harmed myself in any way?

Have I attempted suicide or seriously considered it?

Have I spoken ill of others or harmed their reputation through calumny (saying falsehoods about them) or detraction (revealing faults or other facts that injure another's reputation)?

6. You shall not commit adultery.

For those not married

Have I been sexually active with anyone? Was that person of the opposite sex or the same sex? Was that person married?

Have I used artificial birth control or been sterilized?

Have I engaged in unnatural forms of sex?

Have I engaged in sexual behavior with someone else through the internet or phone?

Have I viewed pornography or lewd material in videos, online, or in printed materials?

Have I been impure with myself by masturbating?

Have I engaged in any activity with the intention of becoming sexually aroused or sexually active, such as impure touching or overly passionate kissing?

Have I used impure language or told impure jokes?

Have I been immodest in dress?

For the married

Was I married outside of the Church without proper permission of the Church? (Ask the priest if you are not sure.)

Have I been faithful to my marriage vows in thought and action?

Have I used artificial birth control or been sterilized?

Have I interrupted intercourse during sex with my spouse in order to avoid a pregnancy?

Have I used reproductive technologies that do not respect the dignity of the life conceived or the integrity of the natural sexual union of husband and wife; for example, in vitro fertilization (IVF)?

Have I engaged in unnatural forms of sex?

Have I engaged in sexual behavior with someone else through the internet or phone?

Have I viewed pornography or lewd material in videos, online, or in printed materials?

Have I been impure with myself by masturbating?

Have I used impure language or told impure jokes?

Have I been immodest in dress?

7. **You shall not steal.**

Have I taken what is not mine?

Have I stolen anything from an employer or employee?

Have I destroyed property belonging to someone else?

Have I knowingly accepted stolen goods?

Have I made restitution for what I have stolen?

Have I given my employer an honest day's work or have I squandered my time?

Have I cheated?

Have I acquired digital media illegally or without paying? Have I copied something illegally?

Jesus teaches us to have a special love for the poor.

Have I neglected those in need or ignored the poor?

Am I generous with the material possessions I have?

Do I assist with the material needs of the Church according to my ability?

8. **You shall not bear false witness against your neighbor.**

Have I sworn falsely?

Have I lied? About serious matters?

Have I gossiped or ruined anyone's good name?

Have I spoken falsehoods about others (calumny)?

Have I revealed information about anyone that should have been kept confidential (detraction)?

9. You shall not desire your neighbor's wife.

Have I deliberately and consciously permitted sexual thoughts about someone to whom I am not married?

Do I try to control my imagination? Do I deliberately entertain impure thoughts?

Do I try to avoid impure media (e.g., books, movies, TV shows)? Have I watched shows, videos, plays, or movies that contain impure scenes with the deliberate intention of watching those impure scenes?

10. You shall not desire your neighbor's goods.

Am I envious of the possessions, talents, and successes of others?

Have I acted out of jealousy of someone's gifts or talents?

You shall love your neighbor as yourself.

Do I love myself as God loves me?

Do I care for my physical, emotional, and spiritual health?

Do I love my neighbor?

Are there persons who I do not love or refuse to love?

Have I ridiculed or humiliated others?

Am I prejudiced?

Do I seek to help and assist others in need?

Do I seriously try to love others as Jesus wants?

Do I forgive from my heart those who have hurt me?

Do I pray for my enemies?

Precepts of the Church

Do I go to Confession at least once a year when I have serious sins to confess?

Do I receive Holy Communion at least once during Easter time?

Do I fast for one hour before receiving communion?

Do I abstain from meat on Fridays during Lent (for those age 14 and over) and fast on Ash Wednesday and Good Friday (for those ages 16–59)?

ACT OF CONTRITION

O MY GOD, I am heartily sorry for having offended Thee, and I detest all my sins because I dread the loss of heaven and the pains of hell; but most of all, because they offend Thee, my God, Who art all good and deserving of all my love. I firmly resolve, with the help of Thy grace, to confess my sins, to do penance and to amend my life. Amen.

HOW TO PRAY THE ROSARY

Most of these prayers can be found at the beginning of Part I. The "O My Jesus" prayer and the Prayers after the Rosary can be found in this section after the Mysteries of the Rosary.

1. Make the *Sign of the Cross* and say *The Apostles' Creed*.

2. Say the *Our Father*.

3. Say 3 *Hail Mary's* (for faith, hope, and charity).

4. Say the *Glory be to the Father*.

5. Announce the First Mystery; then say the *Our Father*.

6. Say 10 *Hail Mary's*.

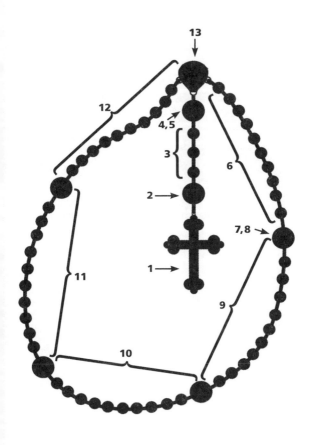

33

7. Say the Glory be to the Father.

8. Say the O My Jesus.

9. Announce the Second Mystery; then say the *Our Father*, 10 *Hail Mary's*, *Glory be*, and *O My Jesus*.

10. Announce the Third Mystery; then say the *Our Father*, 10 *Hail Mary's*, *Glory be*, and *O My Jesus*.

11. Announce the Fourth Mystery; then say the *Our Father*, 10 *Hail Mary's*, *Glory be*, and *O My Jesus*.

12. Announce the Fifth Mystery; then say the *Our Father*, 10 *Hail Mary's*, *Glory be*, and *O My Jesus*.

13. Conclude by saying the *Prayers after the Rosary*.

THE MYSTERIES OF THE ROSARY

To be meditated upon while praying the Rosary.

The Joyful Mysteries
Said on Mondays and Saturdays.

1st Joyful Mystery: The Annunciation

2nd Joyful Mystery: The Visitation

3rd Joyful Mystery: The Nativity

4th Joyful Mystery: The Presentation of Our Lord in the Temple

5th Joyful Mystery: The Finding of Our Lord in the Temple

The Luminous Mysteries
Said on Thursdays.

1st Luminous Mystery: The Baptism in the Jordan

2nd Luminous Mystery: Our Lord's Self-manifestation at the Wedding of Cana

3rd Luminous Mystery: The Proclamation of the Kingdom of God and Call to Conversion

4th Luminous Mystery: The Transfiguration

5th Luminous Mystery: The Institution of the Eucharist

The Sorrowful Mysteries
Said on Tuesdays and Fridays.

1st Sorrowful Mystery: The Agony in the Garden

2nd Sorrowful Mystery: The Scourging at the Pillar

3rd Sorrowful Mystery: The Crowning with Thorns

4th Sorrowful Mystery: The Carrying of the Cross

5th Sorrowful Mystery: The Crucifixion and Death of Our Lord on the Cross

The Glorious Mysteries
Said on Wednesdays and Sundays.

1st Glorious Mystery: The Resurrection of
Our Lord

2nd Glorious Mystery: The Ascension of
Our Lord

3rd Glorious Mystery: The Descent of the
Holy Spirit upon the Apostles

4th Glorious Mystery: The Assumption of
the Blessed Virgin Mary into Heaven

5th Glorious Mystery: The Coronation of
Our Lady as Queen of Heaven and Earth

O MY JESUS

O MY JESUS, forgive us our sins, save
us from the fires of Hell, lead all souls to
Heaven, especially those who are most in
need of Thy mercy.

PRAYERS AFTER THE ROSARY

HAIL, holy Queen, Mother of mercy, our life, our sweetness and our hope! To thee do we cry, poor banished children of Eve. To thee do we send up our sighs, mourning and weeping in this valley of tears. Turn then, Most Gracious Advocate, thine eyes of mercy toward us. And after this our exile, show unto us the blessed Fruit of thy womb, Jesus. O clement, O loving, O sweet Virgin Mary.

V. Pray for us, O holy Mother of God.

R. *That we may be made worthy of the promises of Christ.*

Let Us Pray

O God, Whose only-begotten Son, by His life, death and Resurrection, has purchased for us the rewards of eternal salvation, grant, we beseech Thee, that, meditating upon these Mysteries of the Most Holy Rosary of the Blessed Virgin Mary, we may both imitate what they contain and obtain what they promise. Through the same Christ Our Lord. Amen.

HOW TO PRAY THE DIVINE MERCY CHAPLET

Done using a Rosary.

1. Make the Sign of the Cross.

2. Optional Opening Prayers.

   You expired, Jesus, but the source of life gushed forth for souls, and the ocean of mercy opened up for the whole world. O Fount of Life, unfathomable Divine Mercy, envelop the whole world and empty Yourself out upon us.

   (Repeat three times)

   O Blood and Water, which gushed forth from the Heart of Jesus as a fountain of Mercy for us, I trust in You!

3. *Our Father*, *Hail Mary*, and *The Apostles' Creed* (said on the three beads before the decades begin).

4. *The Eternal Father* (said on all the Our Father beads for the Rosary).

   Eternal Father, I offer you the Body and Blood, Soul and Divinity of Your Dearly Beloved Son, Our Lord, Jesus Christ, in atonement for our sins and those of the whole world.

5. On the Ten Small Beads of Each Decade, say:

   For the sake of His sorrowful Passion, have mercy on us and on the whole world.

6. Conclude with *Holy God* (Repeat three times).
   Holy God, Holy Mighty One, Holy Immortal One, have mercy on us and on the whole world.

7. Repeat for the remaining decades

8. Optional Closing Prayer.

   Eternal God, in whom mercy is endless and the treasury of compassion — inexhaustible, look kindly upon us and

increase Your mercy in us, that in difficult moments we might not despair nor
become despondent, but with great confidence submit ourselves to Your holy
will, which is Love and Mercy itself.

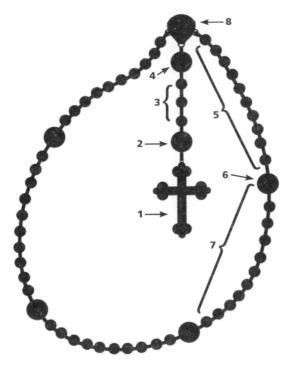

PART III

MARIAN PRAYERS

HAIL MARY

HAIL MARY, full of grace, the Lord is with thee; blessed art thou among women, and blessed is the fruit of thy womb, Jesus. Holy Mary, Mother of God, pray for us sinners, now and at the hour of our death. Amen.

SALVE REGINA (HAIL, HOLY QUEEN)

HAIL, holy Queen, Mother of mercy, our life, our sweetness and our hope! To thee do we cry, poor banished children of Eve. To thee do we send up our sighs, mourning and weeping in this valley of tears. Turn then, Most Gracious Advocate, thine eyes of mercy toward us. And after this our exile, show unto us the blessed Fruit of thy womb, Jesus. O clement, O loving, O sweet Virgin Mary.

LEADER: Pray for us O Holy Mother of God

RESPONSE: That we may be made worthy of the promises of Christ.

THE MEMORARE

REMEMBER, O most gracious Virgin Mary, that never was it known that anyone who fled to thy protection, implored thy help or sought thy intercession was left unaided. Inspired with this confidence, I fly unto thee, O Virgin of virgins, my Mother. To thee do I come, before thee I stand, sinful and sorrowful. O Mother of the Word Incarnate, despise not my petitions, but in thy mercy hear and answer me. Amen.

PRAYERS IN HONOR OF THE SEVEN SORROWS OF THE BLESSED VIRGIN MARY

V. O God, come to my assistance;

R. *O Lord, make haste to help me.*

V. Glory be to the Father . . .

R. *As it was in the beginning . . .*

1. I grieve for thee, O Mary most sorrowful, in the affliction of thy tender heart at *the prophecy of the holy and aged Simeon.* Dear Mother, by thy heart so afflicted, obtain for me the virtue of humility and the Gift of the holy Fear of God. *Hail Mary . . .*

2. I grieve for thee, O Mary most sorrowful, in the anguish of thy most affectionate heart during *the flight into Egypt* and thy sojourn there. Dear Mother, by thy heart so troubled, obtain for me the virtue of generosity, especially toward the poor, and the Gift of Piety. *Hail Mary . . .*

3. I grieve for thee, O Mary most sorrowful, in those anxieties which tried thy troubled heart at *the loss of thy dear Jesus in the Temple*. Dear Mother, by thy heart so full of anguish, obtain for me the virtue of chastity and the Gift of Knowledge. *Hail Mary . . .*

4. I grieve for thee, O Mary most sorrowful, in the consternation of thy heart at *meeting Jesus as He carried His Cross*. Dear Mother, by thy heart so troubled, obtain for me the virtue of patience and the Gift of Fortitude. *Hail Mary . . .*

5. I grieve for thee, O Mary most sorrowful, in the martyrdom which thy generous heart endured in *standing near Jesus in His agony on the Cross*. Dear Mother, by thy afflicted heart, obtain for me the virtue of temperance and the Gift of Counsel. *Hail Mary . . .*

6. I grieve for thee, O Mary most sorrowful, in the wounding of thy compassionate

heart, when *the side of Jesus was struck by the lance before His Body was removed from the Cross*. Dear Mother, by thy heart thus transfixed, obtain for me the virtue of fraternal charity and the Gift of Understanding. *Hail Mary . . .*

7. I grieve for thee, O Mary most sorrowful, for the pangs that wrenched thy most loving heart at *the burial of Jesus*. Dear Mother, by thy heart sunk in the bitterness of desolation, obtain for me the virtue of diligence and the Gift of Wisdom. *Hail Mary . . .*

Let Us Pray

Let intercession be made for us, we beseech Thee, O Lord Jesus Christ, now and at the hour of our death, before the throne of Thy mercy, by the Blessed Virgin Mary, Thy Mother, whose most holy soul was pierced by a sword of sorrow in the hour of Thy bitter Passion, through Thee, O Jesus Christ, Saviour of the world, Who with the Father and the Holy Ghost lives and reigns world without end. Amen.

According to St. Bridget of Sweden (1303-1373), the Blessed Virgin grants the following favors to those who honor her daily by saying seven Hail Marys, while meditating on her tears and sorrows: 1. "I will grant peace to their families." 2. "They will be enlightened about the divine Mysteries." 3. "I will console them in their pains, and I will accompany them in their work." 4. "I will give them as much as they ask for, as long so it does not oppose the adorable Will of my divine Son or the sanctifi-cation of their souls." 5. "I will defend them in their spiritual battles with the infernal enemy, and I will protect them at every instant of their lives." 6. "I will visibly help them at the moment of their death—they will see the face of their mother." 7. "I have obtained this grace from my divine Son, that those who propagate this devotion to my tears and dolors will be taken directly from this earthly life to eternal happiness, since all their sins will be forgiven and my Son will be their eternal consolation and joy."

PRAYER TO OUR LADY OF MT. CARMEL

O MOST Beautiful Flower of Mount Carmel, Fruitful Vine, Splendor of Heaven, Blessed Mother of the Son of God, Immaculate Virgin, assist me in this my necessity. (*Mention your intention.*) O Star of the Sea, help me and show me in this that thou art my Mother.

O Holy Mary, Mother of God, Queen of Heaven and Earth, I humbly beseech thee, from the bottom of my heart, to succour me in this necessity; there are none that can withstand thy power. O, show me in this that thou art my Mother.

O Mary, conceived without sin, pray for us who have recourse to thee. (*3 times*).

Sweet Mother, I place this cause in thy hands. (*3 times*).

It is suggested to offer three times the Our Father, Hail Mary, and Glory Be in thanksgiving.

SALUTATIONS TO MARY

HAIL MARY, Daughter of God the Father!

Hail Mary, Mother of God the Son!

Hail Mary, Spouse of God the Holy Ghost!

Hail Mary, Temple of the Most Blessed Trinity!

Hail Mary, Pure Lily of the Effulgent Trinity!

Hail Mary, Celestial Rose of the ineffable Love of God!

Hail Mary, Virgin pure and humble, of whom the King of Heaven willed to be born and with thy milk to be nourished!

Hail Mary, Virgin of Virgins!

Hail Mary, Queen of Martyrs, whose soul a sword transfixed!

Hail Mary, Lady most blessed unto whom all power in Heaven and earth is given!

Hail Mary, My Queen and my Mother, my Life, my sweetness and my Hope!

Hail Mary, Mother most Amiable!

Hail Mary, Mother most Admirable!

Hail Mary, Mother of Divine Love!

Hail Mary, Immaculate, Conceived without sin!

Hail Mary, Full of Grace, The Lord is with Thee! Blessed art Thou among Women, and Blessed be the Fruit of thy womb, Jesus.

Blessed be thy Spouse, St. Joseph.

Blessed be thy Father, St. Joachim.

Blessed be thy Mother, St. Anne.

Blessed be thy Guardian, St. John.

Blessed be thy Holy Angel, St. Gabriel.

Glory be to God the Father, Who chose thee!

Glory be to God the Son, Who loved thee!

Glory be to God the Holy Spirit, Who espoused thee!

O Glorious Virgin Mary, may all men love and praise thee!

Holy Mary, Mother of God, pray for us and bless us, now and at death, in the Name of Jesus, thy Divine Son! Amen.

MEMORARE TO OUR LADY OF THE SACRED HEART

REMEMBER, Our Lady of the Sacred Heart, the ineffable power which thy Divine Son has given thee over His adorable Heart. Full of confidence in thy merits, we now implore thy protection. O Heavenly Treasurer of the Heart of Jesus, of that Heart which is the inexhaustible source of all graces and which thou dost open when it pleases thee, in order to distribute among men all the treasures of love and mercy, of light and salvation which it contains: grant us, we beseech thee, the favors we request.

(*Mention your requests.*) No, we cannot meet with a refusal, and since thou art our Mother, Our Lady of the Sacred Heart, favorably hear and grant our prayers. Amen.

THE MAGNIFICAT

Words of Our Lady from Luke 1:46-55

MY SOUL doth magnify the Lord, and my spirit hath rejoiced in God my Savior, because He has regarded the humility of His handmaid: for behold, from henceforth all generations shall call me blessed, because He that is mighty hath done great things to me, and holy is His Name. And His mercy is from generation unto generations, to them that fear Him.

He hath showed might in His arm: He hath scattered the proud in the conceit of their heart. He hath put down the mighty from their seat, and hath exalted the humble. He hath filled the hungry with good things, and the rich He hath sent away empty. He hath received Israel His servant, being mindful of His mercy: as He spoke to our fathers, to Abraham and to his seed forever.

PRAYER TO OUR LADY OF GUADALUPE FOR THE CONVERSION OF THE AMERICAS AND OF THE WORLD

O HOLY MARY, Virgin Mother of God, who as Our Lady of Guadalupe didst aid in the conversion of Mexico from paganism in a most miraculous way, we now beseech thee to bring about in these our times the early conversion of our modern world from its present neo-paganism to the One, Holy, Catholic and Apostolic Church of thy divine Son, Jesus Christ, starting in the Americas and extending throughout the entire world, so that soon there may be truly "one fold and one shepherd," with all governments recognizing the reign of thy Son, Jesus Christ the King. This we ask of the Eternal

Father, through Jesus Christ His Son Our Lord and by thy powerful intercession—all for the salvation of souls, the triumph of the Church and peace in the world. Amen.

PRAYER TO OUR LADY OF MENTAL PEACE

O MOTHER of tranquility, Mother of hope, Our Lady of Mental Peace, we reach out to thee for what is needful in our weakness. Teach a searching heart that God's love is unchanging, that human love begins and grows by touching His Love.

Our Lady of Mental Peace, pray for us!

PRAYER TO OUR SORROWFUL MOTHER FOR A FAVOR

MOST holy and afflicted Virgin, Queen of Martyrs, who stood beneath the Cross, witnessing the agony of thy dying Son, look with a mother's tenderness and pity on me, who kneel before thee. To whom shall I have recourse in my needs and miseries if not to thee, O Mother of Mercy? Thou hast drunk so deeply of the chalice of thy Son that thou canst compassionate all our sorrows. I venerate thy sorrows, and I place my request with filial confidence in the sanctuary of thy wounded heart. (*Here mention your request.*)

Present it, I beseech thee, on my behalf to Jesus Christ, through the merits of His own most sacred Passion and Death, together with thine own sufferings at the foot of the Cross. Through the united efficacy of both thy Son's sufferings and thy own, obtain the granting of my petition.

Holy Mary, whose soul was pierced by a sword of sorrow at the sight of the Passion of thy divine Son, intercede for me and obtain for me from Jesus this favor, if it be for His honor and glory and for my good. Amen.

PRAYER TO OUR MOTHER OF PERPETUAL HELP FOR THE CONVERSION OF A SINNER

O MARY, Mother of Perpetual Help, thou know so well the great value of an immortal soul. Thou know what it means, that every soul has been redeemed by the Blood of thy Divine Son. Thou wilt not then despise my prayer if I ask from thee the conversion of a sinner, nay, a great sinner, who is rapidly hurrying on toward eternal ruin. Thou, O good and merciful Mother, know well his (*her*) irregular life. Remember that thou art the Refuge of Sinners; remember that God has given thee power to bring about the conversion of even the most wretched sinners. All that has been done for his (*her*) soul has been unsuccessful; if thou wilt not come to his (*her*) assistance, he (*she*) will go from bad to worse. Obtain for him (*her*) the effectual grace that he (*she*) may be moved and brought back to God and to his (*her*) duties. Send him (*her*), if necessary, temporal calamities and trials, that he (*she*) may enter into himself (*herself*) and put an end to his (*her*) sinful course. Thou, O most merciful Mother, hast converted so many sinners through thine intercession, at the prayer to thee of their friends. Be then also moved by my prayer, and bring this unhappy soul to true conversion of heart.

O Mother of Perpetual Help, deign to show that thou art the Advocate and Refuge of Sinners. So I hope, so may it be. Amen.

A SHORT CONSECRATION TO THE BLESSED VIRGIN MARY

My Queen and my Mother,
I give myself entirely to you;
and to show my devotion to you,
I consecrate to you this day my eyes,
my ears, my mouth, my heart,
my whole being without reserve.
Wherefore, good Mother,

as I am your own,
keep me, guard me,
as your property and possession.
Amen.

PART IV

Saint Prayers

ASPIRATION TO THE HOLY FAMILY

JESUS, Mary and Joseph, I give Thee my heart and my soul.

Jesus, Mary and Joseph, assist me in my last agony.

Jesus, Mary and Joseph, may I breathe forth my soul in peace with Thee.

MEMORARE TO ST. JOSEPH

REMEMBER, O most chaste spouse of the Virgin Mary, that never was it known that anyone who implored your help and sought your intercession were left unassisted. Full of confidence in your power I fly unto you and beg your protection. Despise not O Guardian of the Redeemer my humble supplication, but in your bounty, hear and answer me. Amen.

PRAYER TO ST. JOSEPH TO OBTAIN A SPECIAL FAVOR

O BLESSED Saint Joseph, tenderhearted father, faithful guardian of Jesus, chaste spouse of the Mother of God, we pray and beseech thee to offer to God the Father His Divine Son, bathed in blood on the cross for sinners, and through the thrice-holy Name of Jesus, obtain for us from the Eternal Father the favor we implore. (*Here mention your intention.*)

Appease the Divine anger so justly inflamed by our crimes; beg of Jesus mercy for thy children. Amid the splendors of eternity, forget not the sorrows of those who suffer, those who pray, those who weep. Stay the Almighty arm which smites us, that by thy prayers and those of thy most holy spouse, the Heart of Jesus may be moved to pity and to pardon. Amen.

St. Joseph, pray for us.

PRAYER TO ST. JOSEPH IN A DIFFICULT PROBLEM

O GLORIOUS St. Joseph, thou who hast the power to render possible even things which are considered impossible, come to our aid in our present trouble and distress. Take this important and difficult affair under thy particular protection, that it may end happily. (*Name your request.*)

O dear St. Joseph, all our confidence is placed in thee. Let it not be said that we have invoked thee in vain, and since thou art so powerful with Jesus and Mary, show that thy goodness equals thy power. Amen.

St. Joseph, friend of the Sacred Heart, pray for us.

PRAYER TO ST. JOSEPH FOR PURITY

O GUARDIAN of virgins and holy father St. Joseph, into whose faithful custody Christ Jesus, Innocence Itself, and Mary, Virgin of virgins, were committed, I pray and beseech thee, by these dear pledges, Jesus and Mary, that being preserved from all impurity, I may with spotless mind, pure heart and chaste body ever most chastely serve Jesus and Mary all the days of my life. Amen.

PRAYER TO ST. THOMAS FOR PURITY

Said daily by the members of the Angelic Warfare Confraternity

CHOSEN LILY of innocence, pure
  St. Thomas,

who kept chaste the robe of baptism,
and became an angel in the flesh after being
    girded by two angels,
we (I) implore you to commend us (me) to
    Jesus, the Spotless Lamb,
and to Mary, the Queen of Virgins.
Gentle protector of our (my) purity, ask
    them that we (I),
who wear the holy sign of your victory over
    the flesh,
may also share your purity,
and after imitating you on earth
may at last come to be crowned with you
    among the angels. Amen.

PRAYER TO ST. JUDE

Patron of "Hopeless Cases"

O GLORIOUS APOSTLE St. Jude, faithful
servant and friend of Jesus, the name of the
traitor who delivered thy beloved Master into
the hands of His enemies has caused thee to
be forgotten by many, but the Church honors

and invokes thee universally as the Patron of Hopeless Cases, of things almost despaired of. Pray for me who am so helpless and alone. Make use, I implore thee, of that particular privilege granted to thee to bring visible and speedy help where help was almost despaired of. Come to my assistance in this great need, that I will receive the consolation and succor of Heaven in all my necessities, tribulations and sufferings, but in particular, that . . . (*here make your intention*) and that I may praise God with thee and with all the Saints forever. I promise thee, O blessed St. Jude, to be ever mindful of this great favor and never cease to honor thee as my special and powerful patron, and to do all in my power gratefully to encourage devotion to thee. Amen.

O LUMEN (PRAYER TO ST. DOMINIC)

O Light of the Church, Doctor of Truth, Rose of Patience, Ivory of Chastity, you freely poured forth the waters of wisdom; preacher of grace, unite us with the blessed.

(During Easter time: Alleluia!)

V. Holy Father, Dominic, pray for us
 (During Easter time: Alleluia!)

R. That we may be made worthy of the
 promises of Christ *(During Easter time:
 Alleluia!)*

Let us pray:

Grant, we beseech you, Almighty God, that
we who are weighed down by the burden
of our sins, may be relieved through the
patronage of the Blessed Dominic, Your
Confessor and our Father. Through Christ,
our Lord. Amen

PRAYER TO ST. ANTHONY OF PADUA

*St. Anthony of Padua is invoked in a wide
variety of needs but is especially renowned as
the "Patron of Lost Objects."*

O HOLY ST. ANTHONY, gentlest of
Saints, thy love for God and charity for His
creatures made thee worthy when on earth
to possess miraculous powers. Miracles

waited on thy word, which thou wert ever ready to speak for those in trouble or anxiety. Encouraged by this thought, I implore thee to obtain for me . . . (*Here mention your request.*) The answer to my prayer may require a miracle; even so, thou art the Saint of Miracles. O gentle and loving St. Anthony, whose heart was ever full of human sympathy, whisper my petition into the ears of the sweet Infant Jesus, Who loved to be folded in thy arms, and the gratitude of my heart will ever be thine. Amen.

PRAYER TO ST. THÉRÈSE OF LISIEUX, THE LITTLE FLOWER, FOR VIRTUE AND GRACE

St. Thérèse (1873-1897) promised to assist anyone who called upon her for any reason. "I will spend my Heaven in doing good upon earth." "I will let fall a shower of roses."

O LITTLE FLOWER OF JESUS, ever consoling troubled souls with heavenly graces, in thine unfailing intercession I place my confident trust. From the heart of our divine Saviour, petition the blessings of which I stand in greatest need, especially . . . (*here mention your intention*). Shower upon me thy promised roses of virtue and grace, dear St. Thérèse, so that swiftly advancing in sanctity and perfect love of neighbor, I may someday receive the crown of life eternal. Amen.

PRAYER TO ST. MARTIN DE PORRES

O GLORIOUS St. Martin de Porres, great Saint of the Dominican Order, look down in mercy upon a poor soul who cries out to thee, and deign to come to my aid in this great need, that I may receive the consolation and succor of Heaven in all my necessities, tribulations and sufferings, but in particular . . . (*here mention your intention*). I thank thee, St. Martin de Porres, for all the help that thou hast given me, both now and

in the past, and I promise to be ever grateful
to thee and to make thee known to all who
are in need of thine assistance. Amen.

PRAYER OF ST. FRANCIS OF ASSISI

LORD, make me an instrument of Thy
    peace.
Where there is hatred, let me sow love;
where there is injury, pardon;
where there is doubt, faith;
where there is despair, hope;
where there is darkness, light;
and where there is sadness, joy.
O Divine Master, grant that I may not so
    much seek to be consoled as to console;
to be understood as to understand;
to be loved as to love;
for it is in giving that we receive;
it is in pardoning that we are pardoned;
and it is in dying that we are born to eternal
    life. Amen.

PRAYER OF ST. GERTRUDE THE GREAT (PRAYER FOR THE SOULS IN PURGATORY)

O ETERNAL Father, I offer Thee the Most Precious Blood of Thy Divine Son Jesus, in union with all the Masses said throughout the world today, for all the holy souls in Purgatory, and for sinners everywhere: for sinners in the Universal Church, for those in my own home and for those within my family. Amen.

PRAYER OF ST. ELIZABETH OF THE TRINITY

O MY GOD, Trinity whom I adore, help me to become utterly forgetful of myself so that I may establish myself in you, as changeless and calm as though my soul were already in eternity. Let nothing disturb my peace nor draw me forth from you, O my unchanging God, but at every moment may I penetrate more deeply into the depths of your mystery.

Give peace to my soul; make it your heaven, your cherished dwelling-place and the place of your repose. Let me never leave you there alone, but keep me there, wholly attentive, wholly alert in my faith, wholly adoring and fully given up to your creative action.

O my beloved Christ, crucified for love, I long to be the bride of your heart. I long to cover you with glory, to love you even unto death! Yet I sense my powerlessness and beg you to clothe me with yourself. Identify my soul with all the movements of your soul, submerge me, overwhelm me, substitute yourself for me, so that my life may become a reflection of your life. Come into me as Adorer, as Redeemer and as Savior.

O Eternal Word, utterance of my God, I want to spend my life listening to you, to become totally teachable so that I might learn all from you. Through all darkness, all emptiness, all powerlessness, I want to keep my eyes fixed on you and to remain under your great light. O my Beloved Star, so fascinate me that I may never be able to leave your radiance.

O Consuming Fire, Spirit of Love, overshadow me so that the Word may be, as it were incarnate again in my soul. May I be for him a new humanity in which he can renew all his mystery.

And you, O Father, bend down towards your poor little creature. Cover her with your shadow, see in her only your beloved son in who you are well pleased

O my 'Three', my All, my Beatitude, infinite Solitude, Immensity in which I lose myself, I surrender myself to you as your prey. Immerse yourself in me so that I may be immersed in you until I go to contemplate in your light the abyss of your splendor! Amen.

PRAYER TO ST. ANNE FOR A SPECIAL NEED

O GLORIOUS ST. ANNE—filled with compassion for those who invoke thee and with love for those who suffer—heavily ladened with the weight of my troubles, I cast myself at thy feet and humbly beg of thee to take under thy special protection the present affair which I recommend to thee. (*State your petition.*)

Deign to commend it to thy daughter, the Blessed Virgin Mary, and lay it before the throne of Jesus, so that He may bring it to a happy conclusion. Cease not to intercede for me until my request is granted. Above all, obtain for me the grace of one day beholding my God face to face, and with thee and Mary and all the Saints, of praising and blessing Him for all eternity.

O Good St. Anne, mother of her who is our Life, our Sweetness and our Hope, pray to her for us, and obtain our request. Amen. (*Pray this 3 times.*)

I thank thee, dear St. Anne.

PRAYER TO ST. PEREGRINE— "THE CANCER SAINT"

May be said for oneself or for another.

O GLORIOUS wonder-worker, St. Peregrine, who suffered so patiently with incurable cancer in thy leg and then was healed miraculously by a touch of Our Lord's divine hand, I beg of thee to obtain for me deliverance from the infirmities that afflict my body (*or here name patient . . .*), if this be God's Holy Will. Obtain for me (*him/her*) also a perfect resignation to the sufferings it may please God to send me (*him/her*), so that, imitating our crucified Saviour and His sorrowful Mother, I (*he/she*) may merit eternal glory in Heaven. Amen.

St. Peregrine, pray for us.

CREDO: A CATHOLIC PRAYER BOOK

PRAYER TO ST. GERARD
FOR MOTHERHOOD

Patron of Pregnant Women

O GOOD St. Gerard, powerful patron and protector of mothers and of children yet unborn, to thee do I turn in my hour of anxiety. Of thee do I beg the blessings of a happy motherhood. When all human assistance seems to fail, deign to come to my aid by thy powerful intercession at the throne of Almighty God. Beseech the Divine Author of Life to bless me with offspring, that I may raise up children to God in this life who will be heirs to His heavenly Kingdom in the next. Amen.

PRAYER TO ST. GERARD FOR A
MOTHER WITH CHILD

To be said either for oneself or for another.

O ALMIGHTY and Everlasting God, Who through the operation of the Holy Spirit did prepare the body and soul of the glorious Virgin Mary to be a worthy dwelling place of Thy Divine Son; and through the operation of the same Holy Spirit, did sanctify St. John the Baptist while still in his mother's womb, hearken to the prayers of Thy humble servant who implores Thee, through the intercession of St. Gerard, to protect her (*me*) amidst the dangers of childbearing and to watch over the child with which Thou has deigned to bless her (*me*): that it may be cleansed by the saving water of Baptism, and that, after living a Christian life on earth, both the child and its mother may attain to everlasting bliss in Heaven. Amen.

PRAYER TO ST. GERARD IN THANKSGIVING FOR A SAFE DELIVERY

O GOOD St. Gerard, wonderful Patron of Mothers, deign to offer to God my heartfelt gratitude for the great blessing of motherhood. In my long hours of anxiety, uncertainty and doubt, thy powerful intercession with Jesus my Lord and Mary my Queen was ever my hope. Obtain for me the grace always to turn to thee in similar trials. Help me to inspire other women with confidence in thy most gracious assistance. Aid all of us, that, doing God's holy Will as mothers here on earth, we may merit eternal life in Heaven, through Jesus Christ Our Lord. Amen.

PRAYER IN HONOR OF ST. DYMPHNA

Patroness of Those with Mental and Nervous Disorders

O LORD GOD, Who has graciously chosen St. Dymphna to be the patroness of those afflicted with mental and nervous disorders and has caused her to be an inspiration and a symbol of charity to the thousands who invoke her intercession, grant, through the prayers of this pure, youthful martyr, relief and consolation to all who suffer from these disturbances, and especially to those for whom we now pray. (Here mention oneself or names of others.)

We beg Thee to accept and to satisfy the prayers of St. Dymphna on our behalf. Grant us patience in all our sufferings and resignation to Thy divine Will. Fill us with hope, and if it be in accord with Thy divine plan, bestow upon me (*him, her*) the cure I so earnestly ask for. Through Christ Our Lord. Amen.

PRAYER TO ONE'S PATRON SAINT

GREAT ST. (*Name*), who at my Baptism was chosen as my guardian and under whose patronage I became an adopted child of God and solemnly renounced Satan, his works and allurements, assist me by thy powerful intercession in the fulfillment of these sacred promises. Help me to love God above all things and always to live in the state of grace. Finally, obtain for me the grace of a happy death, so that thou mayest welcome me into Heaven for all eternity. Amen.

PART V

PRAYERS FOR
PARTICULAR TIMES

TRADITIONAL MORNING OFFERING

O Jesus,
through the Immaculate Heart of Mary,
I offer You my prayers, works,
joys and sufferings
of this day for all the intentions
of Your Sacred Heart,
in union with the Holy Sacrifice of the Mass
throughout the world,
in reparation for my sins,
for the intentions of all my relatives and
friends,

and in particular
for the intentions of the Holy Father.
Amen.

THE ANGELUS

The Angelus is traditionally prayed standing, in the morning (6:00 a.m.), at noon and in the evening (6:00 p.m.) throughout the year, except during Paschal Time (Easter Sunday through the Saturday after Pentecost), when the Regina Caeli is prayed instead.

V. The Angel of the Lord declared unto Mary.

R. *And she conceived of the Holy Spirit. Hail Mary . . .*

V. Behold the handmaid of the Lord.

R. *Be it done unto me according to thy word. Hail Mary . . .*

V. And the Word was made Flesh. (*Genuflect.*)

R. *And dwelt among us. (Arise.) Hail Mary . . .*

V. Pray for us, O holy Mother of God.

R. *That we may be made worthy of the promises of Christ.*

Let Us Pray

Pour forth, we beseech Thee, O Lord, Thy grace into our hearts, that we to whom the Incarnation of Christ, Thy Son, was made known by the message of an angel, may by His Passion and Cross be brought to the glory of His Resurrection. Through the same Christ Our Lord. Amen.

THE REGINA CAELI

This prayer is traditionally prayed standing, in the morning (6:00 a.m.), at noon and in the evening (6:00 p.m.), during Paschal Time (from Easter through the evening of the Saturday after Pentecost) instead of The Angelus.

V. Queen of Heaven, rejoice. Alleluia.

R. *For He whom you did merit to bear. Alleluia.*

V. Has risen as He said. Alleluia.

R. *Pray for us to God. Alleluia.*

V. Rejoice and be glad, O Virgin Mary. Alleluia.

R. *For the Lord is truly risen. Alleluia.*

Let Us Pray

O God, Who by the Resurrection of Thy Son, Our Lord Jesus Christ, hast been pleased to give joy to the whole world, grant, we beseech Thee, that through the intercession of the Blessed Virgin Mary, His Mother, we may attain the joys of eternal life. Through the same Christ Our Lord. Amen.

A DAILY CONSECRATION TO THE HOLY SPIRIT

O MOST Holy Spirit, receive the consecration that I make of my entire being. From this moment on, come into every area of my life and into each of my actions. Thou art my Light, my Guide, my Strength and the sole desire of my heart. I abandon myself without reserve to Thy divine action, and I desire to be ever docile to Thine inspirations. O Holy Spirit, transform me with and through Mary into "another Christ Jesus," for the glory of the Father and the salvation of the world. Amen.

PRAYER BEFORE COMMUNION

Composed by St. Thomas Aquinas

ALMIGHTY and Eternal God, behold I come to the sacrament of Your only-begotten Son, our Lord Jesus Christ. As one sick I come to the Physician of life; unclean, to the Fountain of mercy; blind, to the Light of eternal splendor; poor and needy to the Lord of heaven and earth. Therefore, I beg of You, through Your infinite mercy and generosity, heal my weakness, wash my uncleanness, give light to my blindness, enrich my poverty, and clothe my nakedness. May I thus receive the Bread of Angels, the King of

Kings, the Lord of Lords, with such reverence and humility, contrition and devotion, purity and faith, purpose and intention, as shall aid my soul's salvation.

Grant, I beg of You, that I may receive not only the Sacrament of the Body and Blood of our Lord, but also its full grace and power. Give me the grace, most merciful God, to receive the Body of your only Son, our Lord Jesus Christ, born of the Virgin Mary, in such a manner that I may deserve to be intimately united with His mystical Body and to be numbered among His members. Most loving Father, grant that I may behold for all eternity face to face Your beloved Son, whom now, on my pilgrimage, I am about to receive under the sacramental veil, who lives and reigns with You, in the unity of the Holy Spirit, God, world without end. Amen.

PRAYER AFTER COMMUNION

Composed by St. Thomas Aquinas

I THANK YOU, Lord, Almighty Father, Everlasting God, for having been pleased, through no merit of mine, but of Your great mercy alone, to feed me, a sinner, and Your unworthy servant, with the precious Body and Blood of Your Son, our Lord Jesus Christ. I pray that this Holy Communion may not be for my judgment and condemnation, but for my pardon and salvation. Let this Holy Communion be to me an armor of faith and a shield of good will, a cleansing of all vices, and a rooting out of all evil desires. May it increase love and patience, humility and obedience, and all virtues. May it be a firm defense against the evil designs of all my visible and invisible enemies, a perfect quieting of all the desires of soul and body. May this Holy Communion bring about a perfect union with You, the one true God, and at last enable me to reach eternal bliss when

You will call me. I pray that You bring me, a sinner, to the indescribable Feast where You, with Your Son and the Holy Spirit, are to Your saints true light, full blessedness, everlasting joy, and perfect happiness. Through the same Christ our Lord. Amen.

ANIMA CHRISTI

Traditionally said after receiving Holy Communion

SOUL OF CHRIST, sanctify me; Body of
   Christ, save me;

Blood of Christ, inebriate me;
   Water from the side of Christ, wash me.

Passion of Christ, strengthen me;
   O good Jesus, hear me;

Within Thy wounds hide me;
   Suffer me not to be separated from
   Thee.

From the malignant enemy defend me;
   In the hour of my death, call me,

And bid me come to Thee,

That, with Thy Saints, I may praise Thee

Forever and ever. Amen.

PART VI

PRAYERS FOR
PARTICULAR NEEDS

PRAYER TO OVERCOME
BAD HABITS

BEHOLD me, O my God, at Thy feet! I do not deserve mercy, but O, my Redeemer, the blood which Thou hast shed for me encourages me and obliges me to hope for it. How often have I offended Thee, repented, and yet have I again fallen into the same sin.

O my God, I wish to amend, and in order to be faithful to Thee, I will place all my confidence in Thee. I will, whenever I am tempted, instantly have recourse to Thee.

Hitherto, I have trusted in my own promises and resolutions and have neglected to recommend myself to Thee in my temptations. This has been the cause of my repeated failures. From this day forward, be Thou, O Lord, my strength, and thus shall I be able to do all things, for "I can do all things in Him who strengthens me." Amen.

PRAYER AGAINST EVIL THOUGHTS

ALMIGHTY and merciful God, look favorably upon my prayer and free my heart from temptation to evil thoughts, that I may deserve to be accounted a worthy dwelling place of the Holy Spirit. Shed upon my heart the brightness of Thy grace, that I may ever think thoughts worthy of Thy Divine Majesty and that are pleasing to Thee, and ever sincerely love Thee, through Christ Our Lord. Amen.

PRAYER FOR DETACHMENT FROM EARTHLY GOODS

O JESUS, Who did choose a life of poverty and obscurity, grant me the grace to keep my heart detached from the transitory things of this world. Be Thou henceforth my only treasure, for Thou art infinitely more precious than all other possessions. My heart is too solicitous for the vain and fleeting things of earth. Make me always mindful of Thy warning words: "What does it profit a man if he gain the whole world, but suffer the loss of his own soul?" Grant me the grace to keep Thy holy example always before my eyes, that I may despise the nothingness of this world and make Thee the object of all my desires and affections. Amen.

PRAYER TO OVERCOME SLOTH AND LUKEWARMNESS

O MY GOD, I know well that so negligent a life as mine cannot please Thee. I know that by my lukewarmness I have closed the door to the graces which Thou dost desire to bestow upon me. O my God, do not reject me, as I deserve, but continue to be merciful toward me, and I will make great efforts to amend and to arise from this miserable state. In the future I will be more careful to overcome my passions, to follow Thine inspirations, and never through slothfulness will I omit my duties, but will ever strive to fulfill them with greater diligence and fidelity. In short, I will from this time forward do all I can to please Thee and will neglect nothing which I know to be pleasing to Thee.

Since Thou, O my Jesus, hast been so liberal with Thy graces toward me and hast deigned to give Thy Blood and Thy Life for me, I am sorry for having acted with so little generosity toward Thee, Who art worthy of all honor and all love. But O my Jesus, Thou know my weakness. Help me with Thy powerful grace; in Thee I confide. O Immaculate Virgin Mary, help me to overcome myself and to become a Saint. Amen.

PRAYER TO ST. JOSEPH TO OBTAIN A SPECIAL FAVOR

O BLESSED Saint Joseph, tenderhearted father, faithful guardian of Jesus, chaste spouse of the Mother of God, we pray and beseech thee to offer to God the Father His Divine Son, bathed in blood on the cross for sinners, and through the thrice-holy Name of Jesus, obtain for us from the Eternal Father the favor we implore. (*Here mention your intention.*)

Appease the Divine anger so justly inflamed by our crimes; beg of Jesus mercy for thy children. Amid the splendors of eternity, forget not the sorrows of those who suffer, those who pray, those who weep. Stay the Almighty arm which smites us, that by thy prayers and those of thy most holy spouse, the Heart of Jesus may be moved to pity and to pardon. Amen.

St. Joseph, pray for us.

PRAYER TO ST. JOSEPH IN A DIFFICULT PROBLEM

O GLORIOUS St. Joseph, thou who hast the power to render possible even things which are considered impossible, come to our aid in our present trouble and distress. Take this important and difficult affair under thy particular protection, that it may end happily. (*Name your request.*)

O dear St. Joseph, all our confidence is placed in thee. Let it not be said that we have invoked thee in vain, and since thou art so powerful with Jesus and Mary, show that thy goodness equals thy power. Amen.

St. Joseph, friend of the Sacred Heart, pray for us.

PRAYER TO ST. JOSEPH FOR PURITY

O GUARDIAN of virgins and holy father St. Joseph, into whose faithful custody Christ Jesus, Innocence Itself, and Mary, Virgin of virgins, were committed, I pray and beseech thee, by these dear pledges, Jesus and Mary, that being preserved from all impurity, I may with spotless mind, pure heart and chaste body ever most chastely serve Jesus and Mary all the days of my life. Amen.

PRAYER OF ST. THOMAS FOR PURITY

Said daily by the members of the Angelic Warfare Confraternity

DEAR JESUS, I know that every perfect gift, and especially that of chastity, depends on the power of Your providence. Without You a mere creature can do nothing. Therefore, I beg You to defend by Your grace the chastity and purity of my body and soul. And if I have ever sensed or imagined anything that could stain my chastity and purity, blot it out, Supreme Lord of my powers, that I may advance with a pure heart in Your love and service, offering myself on the most pure altar of Your divinity all the days of my life. Amen.

PRAYER FOR HEALTH OF BODY AND SOUL

This prayer includes acts of faith, love and perfect contrition.

O LORD Jesus Christ, Who during Thy brief life on earth went about doing good to all men, be merciful to me in this, my hour of special need. O Divine Physician, Thy tender heart was ever moved at the sight of pain and affliction. I beg of Thee, if it be Thy holy Will, to help me regain my health and strength. Stretch forth Thy hand to all who suffer, whether in mind or in body. Grant to each of us that peace of soul which Thou alone canst give.

I believe that in God there are three Divine Persons—Father, Son, and Holy Spirit.

I believe that God so loved the world that He sent Thee, His only-begotten Son, Who died on the Cross for our salvation.

I believe that God, in His mercy and justice, rewards goodness and punishes evil.

I am truly sorry for all my sins, Dear Lord, because they have offended Thee, Who art Goodness itself.

I love Thee with all my heart, and with Thy help, I will try never to offend Thee again.

Assist me to do all that is necessary to obtain eternal life. Amen.

Jesus, Son of David, have mercy on me!

PRAYER IN TIME OF SICKNESS

O DIVINE Physician, Who always loved to console and heal the sick of body and mind, grant me patience to bear my sufferings. By Thy power, relieve the sharpness of my pain and exhaustion, but above all, kind Jesus, heal the wounds of my soul. And even though I find it hard to pray, yet shall I ever say: Thy Will be done. Amen.

PRAYER FOR A PERSON WHO IS SERIOUSLY ILL

MOST merciful Jesus, the Consolation and Salvation of all who put their trust in Thee, we humbly beseech Thee, by Thy most bitter Passion, grant recovery of health to Thy servant (*Name*), provided this be for his (*her*) soul's welfare, that with us he (*she*) may praise and magnify Thy holy name. But if it be Thy holy will to call him (*her*) out of this world, strengthen him (*her*) in his (*her*) last hour, grant him (*her*) a peaceful death and bring him (*her*) to life everlasting. Amen.

Our Father, Hail Mary, Glory Be.

PRAYER FOR THOSE IN THEIR LAST AGONY

O MOST merciful Jesus, lover of souls, I beseech Thee, by the agony of Thy most Sacred Heart and by the sorrows of Thine Immaculate Mother, cleanse in Thine own blood the sinners of the whole world who are now in their agony and are to die this day. Amen.

Heart of Jesus, Most Merciful Savior, who was once in the agony of death, have pity on the dying. Amen.

PRAYER FOR ETERNAL REST

ETERNAL rest grant unto them, O Lord, and let perpetual light shine upon them. May the souls of all the Faithful departed, through the mercy of God, rest in peace. Amen.

PRAYER FOR A DECEASED PERSON

O GOD, Whose way it is always to have mercy and to spare, we beseech Thee on behalf of the soul of Thy servant (*Name*), whom Thou hast called out of this world: look upon him (*her*) with pity and let him be conducted by the holy Angels to Paradise, his true country. Grant that he who believed in Thee and hoped in Thee may not be left to suffer the pains of the Purgatorial fire, but may be admitted to eternal joys, through Jesus Christ, Thy Son Our Lord, who with Thee and the Holy Spirit, live and reigne world without end. Amen.

Our Father, Hail Mary, Glory Be.

V. Eternal rest grant unto him (*her*), O Lord;

R. *And let perpetual light shine upon him* (her).

V. May he (*she*) rest in peace.

R. *Amen.*

A PRAYER FOR THE DEAD

O GOD, the Creator and Redeemer of all the Faithful, grant unto the souls of Thy departed servants full remission of all their sins, that through the help of our pious supplications they may obtain that pardon which they have always desired, Thou Who livest and reignest world without end. Amen.

V. Eternal rest grant unto them, O Lord.

R. *And let perpetual light shine upon them.*

V. May the divine assistance remain always with us. Amen.

R. *And may the souls of all the Faithful departed, through the mercy of God, rest in peace. Amen.*

A PRAYER FOR OUR DEAR DEPARTED

O GOOD JESUS, Whose loving Heart was ever troubled by the sorrows of others, look with pity on the souls of our dear ones in Purgatory, especially (*Names*). O Thou Who didst "love Thine own," hear our cry for mercy, and grant that those whom Thou hast called from our homes and hearts may soon enjoy everlasting rest in the home of Thy Love in Heaven. Amen.

V. Eternal rest grant unto them, O Lord.

R. *And let perpetual light shine upon them. Amen.*

PRAYER TO ALL THE ANGELS FOR A SPECIAL FAVOR

BLESS the Lord, all ye His Angels! Thou who art mighty in strength and do His Will, intercede for me at the throne of God. By thine unceasing watchfulness, protect me in every danger of soul and body. Obtain for me the grace of final perseverance, so that after this life, I may be admitted to thy glorious company and sing with thee the praises of God for all eternity.

All ye holy Angels and Archangels, Thrones and Dominations, Principalities and Powers and Virtues of Heaven, Cherubim and Seraphim, and especially thou, my dear Guardian Angel, intercede for me and obtain for me the special favor I now ask. (*Name your intention.*)

Offer the Glory Be *three times.*

PRAYER TO ST. ANNE FOR A SPECIAL NEED

O GLORIOUS ST. ANNE—filled with compassion for those who invoke thee and with love for those who suffer—heavily ladened with the weight of my troubles, I cast myself at thy feet and humbly beg of thee to take under thy special protection the present affair which I recommend to thee. (*State your petition.*)

Deign to commend it to thy daughter, the Blessed Virgin Mary, and lay it before the throne of Jesus, so that He may bring it to a happy conclusion. Cease not to intercede for me until my request is granted. Above all, obtain for me the grace of one day beholding my God face to face, and with thee and Mary and all the Saints, of praising and blessing Him for all eternity.

O Good St. Anne, mother of her who is our Life, our Sweetness and our Hope, pray to her for us, and obtain our request. Amen. (*Pray this 3 times.*)

I thank thee, dear St. Anne.

PRAYER TO ST. GERARD FOR MOTHERHOOD

Patron of Pregnant Women

O GOOD St. Gerard, powerful patron and protector of mothers and of children yet unborn, to thee do I turn in my hour of anxiety. Of thee do I beg the blessings of a happy motherhood. When all human assistance seems to fail, deign to come to my aid by thy powerful intercession at the throne of Almighty God. Beseech the Divine Author of Life to bless me with offspring, that I may raise up children to God in this life who will be heirs to His heavenly Kingdom in the next. Amen.

PRAYER TO ST. GERARD FOR A MOTHER WITH CHILD

To be said either for oneself or for another.

O ALMIGHTY and Everlasting God, Who through the operation of the Holy Spirit did prepare the body and soul of the glorious Virgin Mary to be a worthy dwelling place of Thy Divine Son; and through the operation of the same Holy Spirit, did sanctify St. John the Baptist while still in his mother's womb, hearken to the prayers of Thy humble servant who implores Thee, through the intercession of St. Gerard, to protect her (*me*) amidst the dangers of childbearing and to watch over the child with which Thou has deigned to bless her (*me*): that it may be cleansed by the saving water of Baptism, and that, after living a Christian life on earth, both the child and its mother may attain to everlasting bliss in Heaven. Amen.

PART VII

NOVENAS AND LITANIES

Novenas are prayers said once a day for nine successive days.

NOVENA TO THE SACRED HEART OF JESUS

O MY JESUS, Thou hast said: "Truly I say to you, ask and it will be given you, seek and you will find, knock and it will be opened to you." Behold I knock, I seek, and I ask for the grace of (*Here name your request*).

Our Father, Hail Mary, Glory Be.

Sacred Heart of Jesus, I place all my trust in Thee.

O my Jesus, Thou hast said: "Truly I say to you, if you ask anything of the Father in My name, He will give it to you." Behold, in Thy name, I ask the Father for the grace of (*Here name your request*).

Our Father, Hail Mary, Glory Be.

Sacred Heart of Jesus, I place all my trust in Thee.

O my Jesus, Thou hast said: "Truly I say to you, Heaven and earth shall pass away, but My words shall not pass away." Encouraged by Thy infallible words, I now ask for the grace of (*Here name your request*).

Our Father, Hail Mary, Glory Be.

Sacred Heart of Jesus, I place all my trust in Thee.

Let Us Pray

O Sacred Heart of Jesus, for Whom it is

impossible not to have compassion on the afflicted, have pity on us miserable sinners and grant us the grace which we ask of Thee, through the Sorrowful and Immaculate Heart of Mary, Thy tender Mother and ours.

Hail, holy Queen, Mother of mercy, our life, our sweetness and our hope. To thee do we cry, poor banished children of Eve: to thee do we send up our sighs, mourning and weeping in this vale of tears. Turn then, most gracious advocate, thine eyes of mercy toward us, and after this our exile, show unto us the blessed fruit of thy womb, Jesus, O clement, O loving, O sweet Virgin Mary!

V. Pray for us O holy Mother of God.

R. *That we may be made worthy of the promises of Christ.*

V. St. Joseph, foster father of Jesus,

R. *Pray for us.*

Let Us Pray

Pour forth, we beseech Thee, O Lord, Thy

grace into our hearts, that we to whom the Incarnation of Christ Thy Son was made known by the message of an Angel, may by His Passion and Cross be brought to the glory of His Resurrection, through the same Christ Our Lord. Amen.

NOVENA PRAYER TO OUR MOTHER OF PERPETUAL HELP

O MOTHER of Perpetual Help, thou art the dispenser of all the gifts which God grants to us miserable sinners; and for this end He has made thee so powerful, so rich and so bountiful, in order that thou may help us in our misery. Thou art the advocate of the most wretched and abandoned sinners who have recourse to thee. Come to my aid, dearest Mother, for I recommend myself to thee. In thy hands I place my eternal salvation, and to thee do I entrust my soul. Count me among thy most devoted servants; take me under thy protection, and it is enough for me. For if thou wilt protect me, dear Mother, I fear nothing: not from my sins, because thou wilt obtain for me the pardon of them; nor from the devils, because thou art more powerful than all Hell together; nor even from Jesus, my Judge Himself, because by one prayer from thee, He will be appeased. But one thing I fear, that in the hour of temptation, I may neglect to call upon thee and thus perish miserably.

Obtain for me, then, O Mother of Perpetual Help, the pardon of my sins, love for Jesus, final perseverance, and the grace to have recourse to thee always.

Three Hail Marys.

NOVENA PRAYER TO ST. JUDE THADDEUS

MOST HOLY APOSTLE, Saint Jude Thaddeus, faithful servant and friend of Jesus, you bear name of the traitor, who delivered the beloved Master into the hands of His enemies. Yet the Church honors and invokes you universally as the patron of hopeless cases and things despaired. Pray for me! Make use, I implore you, of that particular privilege accorded to you to bring visible and speedy help where help is almost despaired. Come to my assistance in this great need that I may receive the consolation and support of heaven in all my necessities, evils, and sufferings: particularly...*(State Your Request)*

... and that I may bless God with you and all the elect throughout eternity. I promise you, O blessed Saint Jude, to be ever mindful of this great favor and I will never cease to honor you as my special and powerful patron and to do all in my power to encourage devotion to you.

V. Saint Jude, Apostle of Hope:

R. Pray for us!

NOVENA PRAYER TO ST. THÉRÈSE

LITTLE Thérèse of the Child Jesus, please pick for me a rose from the heavenly gardens and send it to me as a message of love. O Little Flower of Jesus, ask God today to grant the favors I now place with confidence in your hands . . . (*Mention your requests*).

St. Thérèse, help me to always believe, as you did, in God's great love for me, so that I might imitate your "Little Way" each day. Amen.

POWERFUL NOVENA PRAYER TO THE INFANT JESUS

For Cases of Urgent Need

In cases of great urgency, a novena of nine hours may be made instead of nine days. The prayers should, if possible, be repeated at the same part of the hour, every hour for nine consecutive hours.

O JESUS, Who has said, "Ask and you shall receive, seek and you shall find, knock and it shall be opened unto you," through the intercession of Mary, Thy most holy Mother, I knock, I seek, I ask that my prayer will be granted. (*Mention your request.*)

O Jesus, Who has said, "All that you ask of the Father in My Name He will grant you," through the intercession of Mary, Thy most holy Mother, I humbly and urgently ask Thy Father in Thy Name that my prayer will be granted. (*Mention your request.*)

O Jesus, Who hast said, "Heaven and earth shall pass away, but My word shall not pass away," through the intercession of Mary, Thy most holy Mother, I feel confident that my prayer will be granted. (*Mention your request.*)

(*Then pray the following prayer of thanksgiving.*)

I PROSTRATE myself before Thy holy image, O most gracious Infant Jesus, to offer Thee my most fervent thanks for the blessings Thou hast bestowed upon me.

I shall incessantly praise Thine ineffable mercy and confess that Thou alone art my God, my Helper and my Protector. Henceforth my entire confidence shall be placed in Thee! Everywhere I shall proclaim aloud Thy mercy and generosity, so that Thy great love and the great deeds which Thou dost perform through this miraculous image may be acknowledged by all. May devotion to Thy Holy Infancy increase more and more in the hearts of all Christians, and may all who experience Thine assistance persevere with me in showing unceasing gratitude to Thy most holy infancy, to which be praise and glory forever. Amen.

LITANY OF THE SACRED HEART OF JESUS

Lord, have mercy on us.
Christ, have mercy on us.
Lord, have mercy on us. Christ, hear us.
Christ, graciously hear us.

God the Father of Heaven,

Have mercy on us.

God the Son, Redeemer of the world,

Have mercy on us.

God the Holy Ghost,

Have mercy on us.

Holy Trinity, One God,

Have mercy on us.

God the Father of Heaven, *have mercy on us.*

God the Son, Redeemer of the world, *have mercy on us.*

God, the Holy Spirit, *etc.*

Holy Trinity, One God,

Heart of Jesus, Son of the Eternal Father,

Heart of Jesus, formed by the Holy Spirit in the womb of the Virgin Mother,

Heart of Jesus, substantially united to the Word of God,

Heart of Jesus, of Infinite Majesty,

Heart of Jesus, Sacred Temple of God,

Heart of Jesus, Tabernacle of the Most High,

Heart of Jesus, House of God and Gate of Heaven,

Heart of Jesus, burning furnace of charity,

Heart of Jesus, abode of justice and love,

Heart of Jesus, full of goodness and love,

Heart of Jesus, abyss of all virtues,

Heart of Jesus, most worthy of all praise,

Heart of Jesus, king and center of all hearts,

Heart of Jesus, in whom are all treasures of wisdom and knowledge,

Heart of Jesus, in whom dwells the fullness of divinity,

Heart of Jesus, in whom the Father was well pleased,

Heart of Jesus, of whose fullness we have all received,

Heart of Jesus, desire of the everlasting hills,

Heart of Jesus, patient and most merciful,

Heart of Jesus, enriching all who invoke Thee,

Heart of Jesus, fountain of life and holiness,

Heart of Jesus, propitiation for our sins,

Heart of Jesus, loaded down with opprobrium,

Heart of Jesus, bruised for our offenses,

Heart of Jesus, obedient to death,

Heart of Jesus, pierced with a lance,

Heart of Jesus, source of all consolation,

Heart of Jesus, our life and resurrection,

Heart of Jesus, our peace and our reconciliation,

Heart of Jesus, victim for our sins

Heart of Jesus, salvation of those who trust in Thee,

Heart of Jesus, hope of those who die in Thee,

Heart of Jesus, delight of all the Saints,

Lamb of God, Who takest away the sins of the world,

Spare us, O Lord.

Lamb of God, Who takest away the sins of the world,

Graciously hear us, O Lord.

Lamb of God, Who takest away the sins of the world,

Have mercy on us.

LITANY OF THE BLESSED VIRGIN MARY

(The Litany of Loreto)

Lord, have mercy on us.

Christ, have mercy on us.

Lord, have mercy on us. Christ, hear us.

Christ, graciously hear us.

God the Father of Heaven,

Have mercy on us.

God the Son, Redeemer of the world,

Have mercy on us.

God the Holy Ghost,

Have mercy on us.

Holy Trinity, One God,

Have mercy on us.

Holy Mary, *pray for us.*

Holy Mother of God, *pray for us.*

Holy Virgin of virgins, *etc.*

Mother of Christ,

Mother of divine grace,

Mother most pure,

Mother most chaste,

Mother inviolate,

Mother undefiled,
Mother most amiable,
Mother most admirable,
Mother of good counsel,
Mother of our Creator,
Mother of our Saviour,
Virgin most prudent,
Virgin most venerable,
Virgin most renowned,
Virgin most powerful,
Virgin most merciful,
Virgin most faithful,
Mirror of Justice,
Seat of Wisdom,
Cause of our Joy,
Spiritual Vessel,
Vessel of Honor,
Singular Vessel of Devotion,
Mystical Rose,
Tower of David,
Tower of Ivory,
House of Gold,
Ark of the Covenant,

Gate of Heaven,

Morning Star,

Health of the Sick,

Refuge of Sinners,

Comforter of the Afflicted,

Help of Christians,

Queen of Angels,

Queen of Patriarchs,

Queen of Prophets,

Queen of Apostles,

Queen of Martyrs,

Queen of Confessors,

Queen of Virgins,

Queen of all Saints,

Queen Conceived without Original Sin,

Queen Assumed into Heaven,

Queen of the Most Holy Rosary,

Queen of Families,

Queen of Peace,

Lamb of God, Who takest away the sins of the world,

Spare us, O Lord.

Lamb of God, Who takest away the sins of the world,

Graciously hear us, O Lord.

Lamb of God, Who takest away the sins of the world,

Have mercy on us.

V. Pray for us, O holy Mother of God,

R. *That we may be made worthy of the promises of Christ.*

Let Us Pray

Grant, we beseech Thee, O Lord God, that we Thy servants may enjoy perpetual health of mind and body, and by the glorious intercession of the Blessed Mary, ever Virgin, be delivered from present sorrow and enjoy everlasting happiness. Through Christ Our Lord. Amen.

LITANY OF ST. JOSEPH

Lord, have mercy on us.
Christ, have mercy on us.
Lord, have mercy on us. Christ, hear us.
Christ, graciously hear us.
God the Father of Heaven,
Have mercy on us.
God the Son, Redeemer of the world,
Have mercy on us.
God the Holy Spirit,
Have mercy on us.
Holy Trinity, One God,
Have mercy on us.
Holy Mary, *pray for us.*
St. Joseph, *pray for us.*
Renowned Offspring of David, *etc.*
Light of Patriarchs,
Spouse of the Mother of God,
Chaste Guardian of the Virgin,
Foster Father of the Son of God,
Diligent Protector of Christ,
Head of the Holy Family,
Joseph most just,

Joseph most chaste,

Joseph most prudent,

Joseph most strong,

Joseph most obedient,

Joseph most faithful,

Mirror of Patience,

Lover of Poverty,

Model of Artisans,

Glory of domestic life,

Guardian of Virgins,

Pillar of Families,

Solace of the Afflicted,

Hope of the Sick,

Patron of the Dying,

Terror of Demons,

Protector of Holy Church,

Lamb of God, Who takest away the sins of the world,

> *Spare us, O Lord!*

Lamb of God, Who takest away the sins of the world,

> *Graciously hear us, O Lord!*

Lamb of God, Who takest away the sins of the world,

Have mercy on us.

V. He made him the lord of His household.

R. *And prince over all His possessions.*

Let Us Pray

O God, Who in Thine ineffable Providence didst vouchsafe to choose Blessed Joseph to be the spouse of Thy most holy Mother, grant, we beseech Thee, that we may have for our advocate in Heaven him whom we venerate as our protector on earth, Who livest and reignest world without end. Amen.

LITANY OF THE SAINTS

Lord, have mercy on us.

Christ, have mercy on us.

Lord, have mercy on us. Christ, hear us.

Christ, graciously hear us.

God the Father of Heaven,

Have mercy on us.

God the Son, Redeemer of the world,

Have mercy on us.
God the Holy Spirit,
Have mercy on us.
Holy Trinity, One God,
Have mercy on us.
Holy Mary, *pray for us.*
Holy Mother of God, *pray for us.*
Holy Virgin of virgins, *etc.*
St. Michael,
St. Gabriel,
St. Raphael,
All you Holy Angels and Archangels,
St. John the Baptist,
St. Joseph,
All you Holy Patriarchs and Prophets,
St. Peter,
St. Paul,
St. Andrew,
St. James,
St. John,
St. Thomas,
St. James,
St. Philip,

St. Bartholomew,

St. Matthew,

St. Simon,

St. Jude,

St. Matthias,

St. Barnabas,

St. Luke,

St. Mark,

All you holy Apostles and Evangelists,

All you holy Disciples of the Lord,

All you holy Innocents,

St. Stephen,

St. Lawrence,

St. Vincent,

Sts. Fabian and Sebastian,

Sts. John and Paul,

Sts. Cosmas and Damian,

All you holy Martyrs,

St. Sylvester,

St. Gregory,

St. Ambrose,

St. Augustine,

St. Jerome,

St. Martin,
St. Nicholas,
All you holy Bishops and Confessors,
All you holy Doctors,
St. Anthony,
St. Benedict,
St. Bernard,
St. Dominic,
St. Francis,
All you holy Priests and Levites,
All you holy Monks and Hermits,
St. Mary Magdalene,
St. Agatha,
St. Lucy,
St. Agnes,
St. Cecilia,
St. Anastasia,
St. Catherine,
St. Clare,
All you holy Virgins and Widows,
All you holy Saints of God,
Lord, be merciful, *Lord, save your people.*
From all evil, *Lord, save your people.*

From all sin, *etc.*

From your wrath,

From a sudden and unprovided death,

From the snares of the devil,

From anger, hatred, and all ill-will,

From the spirit of uncleanness,

From lightning and tempest,

From the scourge of earthquake,

From plague, famine, and war,

From everlasting death,

By the mystery of your holy Incarnation,

By your Coming,

By your Birth,

By your Baptism and holy fasting,

By your Cross and Passion,

By your Death and Burial,

By your holy Resurrection,

By your wonderful Ascension,

By the coming of the Holy Spirit,

On the day of judgment,

Be merciful to us sinners, *Lord, hear our prayer.*

That you will spare us, *Lord, hear our prayer.*

That you will pardon us, etc.

That it may please you to bring us to true penance,

Guide and protect your holy Church,

Preserve in holy religion the Pope, and all those in holy Orders,

Humble the enemies of holy Church,

Give peace and unity to the whole Christian people,

Bring back to the unity of the Church all those who are straying, and bring all unbelievers to the light of the Gospel,

Strengthen and preserve us in your holy service,

Raise our minds to desire the things of heaven,

Reward all our benefactors with eternal blessings,

Deliver our souls from eternal damnation, and the souls of our brethren, relatives, and benefactors,

Give and preserve the fruits of the earth,

Grant eternal rest to all the faithful departed,

That it may please You to hear and heed us,
  Jesus, Son of the Living God,

Lamb of God, Who takest away the sins of
  the world,

Spare us, O Lord!

Lamb of God, Who takest away the sins of
  the world,

Graciously hear us, O Lord!

Lamb of God, Who takest away the sins of
  the world,

Have mercy on us.

Christ, hear us,

Christ, graciously hear us

Lord Jesus, hear our prayer.

Lord Jesus, hear our prayer.

Lord, have mercy on us.

Lord, have mercy on us.

Christ, have mercy on us.

Christ, have mercy on us.

Lord, have mercy on us.

Lord, have mercy on us.

LITANY OF DOMINICAN SAINTS

Lord, have mercy on us.
Christ, have mercy on us.
Lord, have mercy on us. Christ hear us.
Christ, graciously hear us.
God the Father of heaven,
Have mercy on us.
God the Son, Redeemer of the world,
Have mercy on us.
God the Holy Spirit,
Have mercy on us.
Holy Trinity, one God,
Have mercy on us.

Holy Mary,
Pray for us. (repeat after each line)
Holy Mother of God,
Holy Virgin of virgins,
St. Michael,
St. Gabriel,
St. Raphael,
St. Joseph,
St. John the Baptist,

All you holy angels and archangels,
All you holy patriarchs and prophets,
All you holy apostles and evangelists,
All you holy martyrs,
All you holy virgins and widows,
All you holy men and women,

Bl. Jane of Aza,
Bl. Reginald of Orleans,
Holy Father Dominic,
Bl. Bertrand,
Bl. Mannes,
Bl. Diana,
Bl. Jordan of Saxony,
Bl. Ceslaus,
St. Peter of Verona,
St. Hyacinth,
Bl. Sadoc and Companions,
Bl. Giles,
St. Margaret of Hungary,
Bl. Bartholomew of Vicenza,
St. Thomas Aquinas,
St. Raymond of Peñyafort,

Bl. Innocent,

St. Albert the Great,

Bl. John of Vercelli,

Bl. Amata,

Bl. Cecilia,

Bl. Emily,

St. Agnes of Montepulciano,

Bl. Margaret of Castello,

Bl. Imelda,

Bl. Margaret Ebner,

Bl. Henry Suso,

St. Catherine of Siena,

Bl. Raymond of Capua,

St. Vincent Ferrer,

Bl. John Dominic,

Bl. Peter of Castello,

Bl. John of Fiesole,

St. Antoninus,

Bl. Osanna of Mantua,

St. Pius,

St. John of Cologne and Companions,

St. Louis Bertrand,

St. Catherine de Ricci,

St. Rose of Lima,

St. Dominic Ibáñez and Companions,

Bl. Agnes of Jesus,

St. Lawrence Ruiz and Companions,

St. Martin de Porres,

St. Francis de Capillas and Companions,

St. Juan Macias,

St. Louis de Montfort,

St. Vincent Liem,

Bl. Marie Poussepin,

St. Ignatius Delgado and Companions,

St. Dominic An-Kham,

Bl. Hyacinth Cormier,

Bl. Pier Giorgio Frassati,

Bl. Bartolo Longo,

All you holy Dominicans,

Lamb of God, you take away the sins of the world,
Spare us, O Lord.
Lamb of God, you take away the sins of the world,
Graciously hear us, O Lord.

Lamb of God, you take away the sins of the world,
Have mercy on us.

Pray for us, all you Dominican Saints and Blesseds,
That we may be worthy of the promises of Christ.

Let Us Pray.

O God, source of all holiness, you have enriched your Church with many gifts in the saints of the Order of Preachers. By following the example of our brothers and sisters, may we come to enjoy their company for ever in the kingdom of our Lord Jesus Christ, your Son, who lives and reigns with you and the Holy Spirit, one God forever and ever. Amen.

— PART VIII —

OTHER PRAYERS

PRAYER BEFORE A CRUCIFIX

BEHOLD, O kind and most sweet Jesus, before Thy face I humbly kneel, and with the most fervent desire of my soul, I pray and beseech Thee to impress upon my heart lively sentiments of faith, hope and charity, true contrition for my sins and a firm purpose of amendment, while with deep affection and grief of soul, I ponder within myself, mentally contemplating Thy five most precious wounds, having before my eyes the words which David the Prophet spoke concerning Thee: "They have pierced

my hands and my feet; they have numbered
all my bones." (Psalm 21:17-18).

Aspirations for any Occasion

Most Sacred Heart of Jesus, have mercy on
us!

My Jesus, I trust in Thee!

THE DIVINE PRAISES

*Traditionally recited publicly at the end of
Benediction of the Blessed Sacrament, just
before the Host is returned to the tabernacle. It
may be recited privately at any time as an act
of praise and thanksgiving.*

BLESSED be God.
Blessed be His Holy Name.
Blessed be Jesus Christ, true God and true
    man.
Blessed be the Name of Jesus.
Blessed be His Most Sacred Heart.
Blessed be His Most Precious Blood.

Blessed be Jesus in the Most Holy Sacrament of the Altar.

Blessed be the Holy Spirit, the Paraclete.

Blessed be the great Mother of God, Mary most holy.

Blessed be her holy and Immaculate Conception.

Blessed be her glorious Assumption.

Blessed be the name of Mary, Virgin and Mother.

Blessed be St. Joseph, her most chaste spouse.

Blessed be God, in His Angels and in His Saints.

PRAYER FOR THE SEVEN GIFTS OF THE HOLY SPIRIT

O LORD JESUS CHRIST, Who before ascending into Heaven did promise to send the Holy Spirit to finish Thy work in the souls of Thine Apostles and Disciples, deign to grant the same Holy Spirit to me, that

He may perfect in my soul the work of Thy grace and Thy love. Grant me the spirit of wisdom, that I may despise the perishable things of this world and aspire only after the things that are eternal; the spirit of understanding, to enlighten my mind with the light of Thy divine truth; the spirit of counsel, that I may ever choose the surest way of pleasing God and gaining Heaven; the spirit of fortitude, that I may bear my cross with Thee and that I may overcome with courage all the obstacles that oppose my salvation; the spirit of knowledge, that I may know God and know myself and grow perfect in the science of the Saints; the spirit of piety, that I may find the service of God sweet and amiable; the spirit of fear, that I may be filled with a loving reverence towards God and may dread in any way to displease Him. Mark me, dear Lord, with the sign of Thy true disciples, and animate me in all things with Thy Spirit. Amen.

PRAYER FOR PRIESTS

O JESUS, Eternal Priest, keep all Thy priests within the shelter of Thy Sacred Heart, where none may harm them. Keep unstained their anointed hands, which daily touch Thy Sacred Body. Keep unsullied their lips purpled with Thy Precious Blood.

Keep pure and unearthly their hearts sealed with the sublime marks of Thy glorious priesthood. Let Thy holy love surround them and shield them from the world's contagion. Bless their labors with abundant fruit, and may the souls to whom they have ministered here below be their joy and consolation and in Heaven their beautiful and everlasting crown. Amen.

O Mary, Queen of the clergy, pray for us, and obtain for us a number of holy priests.

PRAYER FOR DIRECTION IN THE CHOICE OF A STATE OF LIFE

O MERCIFUL Creator, every good and perfect gift, both of nature and of grace, comes down to us from your provident hand. You fill the earth with your goodness and manifest your glory in a variety of creatures. No one creature can exhaust your abundance, and so you speak many into existence that we might come to know better the vast riches of your boundless love.

Lord God, you have destined that each human person tell something unique of your divine life, and you stir up within me the virtuous desires to endeavor this sublime calling. In prayer and sacrament, you make known your will and you offer to each the capacity to recognize your voice as you heal, purify, and strengthen their resolve. Strengthen within me the desire to embrace and persevere in my vocation, that casting aside every weight and sin, I may run unburdened to the heart of your will for me.

I renounce most sincerely every other wish than to fulfill Thy designs on my soul, whatever they may be, and I beseech Thee to grant me that grace which, by imbibing the true spirit of a Christian, will enable me to qualify myself for any state of life to which Thine adorable Providence may call me. O my God, whenever it may become my duty to make a choice, do Thou be my Light and my Counsel, and mercifully make known to me the way wherein I should walk, for I have lifted up my soul to Thee. Preserve me from the suggestions of my own self-love, or worldly prudence, in prejudice to Thy holy inspirations. Let Thy good Spirit lead me into the right way, and let Thine adorable providence place me where all things may be most conducive to Thy glory and to the salvation of souls. Amen.

THE JESUS PRAYER

LORD JESUS Christ, Son of the living God, have mercy on me, a sinner.

PART IX

LISTS AND REFERENCES

MORAL VIRTUES (CARDINAL VIRTUES)

- Prudence
- Justice
- Temperance
- Fortitude

THEOLOGICAL VIRTUES

- Faith
- Hope
- Charity

GIFTS OF THE HOLY SPIRIT

- Knowledge
- Understanding
- Wisdom
- Counsel
- Fear of the Lord (Awe, Reverence)
- Piety
- Fortitude

TEN COMMANDMENTS

1. I am the LORD your God. You shall worship the Lord your God and Him only shall you serve.

2. You shall not take the name of the Lord your God in vain.

3. Remember to keep holy the Sabbath day.

4. Honor your father and your mother.

5. You shall not kill.

6. You shall not commit adultery.

7. You shall not steal.

8. You shall not bear false witness against your neighbor.

9. You shall not covet your neighbor's wife.

10. You shall not covet your neighbor's goods.

BEATITUDES

1. Blessed are the poor in spirit, for theirs is the kingdom of heaven.

2. Blessed are the meek, for they shall possess the earth.

3. Blessed are they who mourn, for they shall be comforted.

4. Blessed are they who hunger and thirst for justice, for they shall be satisfied.

5. Blessed are the merciful, for they shall obtain mercy.

6. Blessed are the pure of heart, for they shall see God.

7. Blessed are the peacemakers, for they shall be called children of God.

8. Blessed are they who suffer persecution for justice sake, for theirs is the kingdom of heaven.

PRECEPTS OF THE CHURCH AND THEIR EXPLANATION (CCC 2041–43)

1st Precept: You shall attend Mass on Sundays and holy days of obligation and rest from servile labor.

2nd Precept: You shall confess your sins at least once a year.

3rd Precept: You shall receive the sacrament of the Eucharist at least during the Easter season.

4th Precept: You shall observe the days of

fasting and abstinence established by the Church.

5th Precept: You shall help to provide for the needs of the Church.

The precepts of the Church are set in the context of a moral life bound to and nourished by liturgical life. The obligatory character of these positive laws decreed by the pastoral authorities is meant to guarantee to the faithful the very necessary minimum in the spirit of prayer and moral effort, in the growth in love of God and neighbor:

The first precept ("You shall attend Mass on Sundays and holy days of obligation and rest from servile labor") requires the faithful to sanctify the day commemorating the resurrection of the Lord as well as the principal liturgical feasts honoring the mysteries of the Lord, the Blessed Virgin Mary, and the saints; in the first place, by participating in the Eucharistic celebration, in which the Christian community is gathered, and

CREDO: A CATHOLIC PRAYER BOOK

by resting from those works and activities which could impede such a sanctification of these days.

The second precept ("You shall confess your sins at least once a year") ensures preparation for the Eucharist by the reception of the sacrament of Reconciliation, which continues Baptism's work of conversion and forgiveness.

The third precept ("You shall receive the sacrament of the Eucharist at least during the Easter season") guarantees as a minimum the reception of the Lord's Body and Blood in connection with the Paschal feasts, the origin and center of the Christian liturgy.

The fourth precept ("You shall observe the days of fasting and abstinence established by the Church") ensures the times of ascesis and penance which prepare us for the liturgical feasts and help us acquire mastery over our instincts and freedom of heart.

The fifth precept ("You shall help to provide

for the needs of the Church") means that the faithful are obliged to assist with the material needs of the Church, each according to his own ability.

HOLY DAYS OF OBLIGATION

In addition to Sunday, the days to be observed as holy days of obligation in the Latin Rite dioceses of the United States of America are as follows:

- January 1, the solemnity of Mary, Mother of God

- Thursday of the Sixth Week of Easter, the solemnity of the Ascension*

- August 15, the solemnity of the Assumption of the Blessed Virgin Mary

- November 1, the solemnity of All Saints

- December 8, the solemnity of the Immaculate Conception

- December 25, the solemnity of the Nativity of Our Lord Jesus Christ

Whenever January 1, the solemnity of Mary, Mother of God, or August 15, the solemnity of the Assumption, or November 1, the solemnity of All Saints, falls on a Saturday or on a Monday, the precept to attend Mass is abrogated (rescinded).

Whenever December 8, the solemnity of the Immaculate Conception, falls on a Sunday, the feast is transferred to Monday, December 9 and the precept to attend Mass is abrogated.

*Some dioceses have transferred the solemnity of the Ascension from Thursday of the Sixth Week of Easter to the Seventh Sunday of Easter.

Source: USCCB Complementary Norms, Canon 1246, §2 - Holy Days of Obligation

FASTING AND ABSTINENCE

In U.S. dioceses

Penance and self-denial are necessary for the Christian life. In her role of teaching and governing, the Church sets forth specific standards that all Catholics are bound to observe as a minimum of voluntary penance.

Fasting: Restricting how much food you eat

For members of the Latin Catholic Church, the norms on fasting are obligatory from age 18 until age 59. When fasting, a person is permitted to eat one full meal, as well as two smaller meals that together are not equal to a full meal. No food should be taken between meals.

Abstinence: Refraining from eating meat

Fridays during Lent are obligatory days of abstinence; that is, refraining from eating meat. The norms concerning abstinence from meat are binding upon members of the Latin Catholic Church from age 14 onwards.

Ash Wednesday and Good Friday are obligatory days of **both fasting and abstinence** for Catholics.

If possible, the fast on Good Friday is continued until the Easter Vigil (on Holy Saturday night) as the "paschal fast" to honor the suffering and death of the Lord Jesus and to prepare ourselves to share more fully and to celebrate more readily his resurrection.

Fridays throughout the Year (not during Lent)
The requirement to abstain from meat on Fridays was at one time required throughout the whole of the year. In the dioceses of the United States, some form of penance is obligatory on Fridays outside of Lent, but abstinence from meat is no longer required. However, Catholics are strongly encouraged to maintain the practice of abstaining from meat on Fridays throughout the entire year. If this abstinence is not practiced, then some other suitable form of penance should be undertaken. Alternatives to abstinence that

are particularly recommended are refraining from alcoholic beverages or performing corporal or spiritual works of mercy.

Eucharistic Fast: To prepare for the worthy reception of Eucharist, Catholics must fast for one hour before receiving Holy Communion (with the exception of water and medicine).

For more information see: USCCB Pastoral Statement on Penance and Abstinence, 1966.